A Fragile Light

A Fragile Light

Poems

Lois Parker Edstrom

MoonPath Press

Copyright © 2025 Lois Parker Edstrom
All rights reserved.

No part of this publication may be reproduced, distributed, or transmitted in any form or by any means whatsoever without written permission from the publisher, except in the case of brief excerpts for critical reviews and articles. All inquiries should be addressed to MoonPath Press.

Poetry
ISBN 979-8-9899488-1-9

Cover Photo: Emily Gibson

Author photo: Mel Edstrom

Book design by Tonya Namura, using Corporate A Condensed

MoonPath Press, an imprint of Concrete Wolf Poetry Series,
is dedicated to publishing the finest poets
living in the U.S. Pacific Northwest.

MoonPath Press
c/o Concrete Wolf
PO Box 2220
Newport, OR 97365-0163

MoonPathPress@gmail.com

http://MoonPathPress.com

*For
Brian and Deb
Brent and Jennifer
With love and admiration*

Contents

I

A Quiet Tune	5
Trimming the Sails	6
Below the Surface	7
Voices	8
Of Sea and Sky	9
Viewpoint	10
The Wind's Moods	11
Winter Sailing	12
Spring Storm	13
Whale Song	14
Unbroken Line	15

II

Reverie	19
The Grace of Uncertainty	20
Beyond Silence	21
Airy Flights of Blue	22
Moat of Tears	23
Storm	24
Gift of Work	25
Prescription	26
Penn Cove	27
Untold Stories	28

III

White Peony	31
Pioneer Cemetery	32
Uncle Bud	33

Blue Stilly	34
Homesickness	35
The Stone House	36
Breathe	37
Ring of Fire	38
Tradition	39
The Blue Hour	40
Madrone	41
Leaves in a Windstorm	42
Last Hours	43
Soft Heart	44
Sunlight and Shadow	45

IV

Next Note	49
Band of Counterparts	50
Hollow	51
Melodies of Wood	52
The Banjolele	53
Night Music	54
Keeping Us Humble	55
Jazz Trio	56
Island Spring	57

V

Original Recyclers	61
Camano Island Art Tour	62
Friendship	63
Big Bee	64
The Host	65
Through Barn Doors	66

Illusions	67
Autumn Crocuses	68
Living in the Country	69
Tales from an Apple Orchard	70
Imaginary Friends	71
Desperate Measures	72
The Sick Tray	73
A Numbers Game	74
What We Leave Behind	75
From Woods and Field	76

Coda

A Fragile Light	81
Gratitude	83
About the Author	85

A Fragile Light

I

Sometimes in the winds of change we find our true direction.
—*Unknown*

A Quiet Tune

Whidbey Island

Along the roadways, beach peas riot and ocean spray
rises in frothy clouds. Wild roses border fields
suffused with the contentment of grazing cows

and morning light polishes the leaves of willows,
dances across the prairie to where the bluff drops
down to the sea.

An incoming tide sighs against the shore,
a haunting rhythm that fills me with dreaming,
and I can't quite decide how to answer

the mysterious call. What are we to do
with such abundance? It can't be a matter
of merit, but perhaps of learning to receive.

Now fog drifts into the inlet softening sounds
and expectations, and stillness hums its quiet tune.

Trimming the Sails

Galadriel, the Lady of Light, bears us
out of the marina and through the channel

heading for the San Juan Islands where currents
run strong and winds are moody.

Clearing the last buoy, we raise the mainsail,
then clubfoot and jib, quarter into the wind.

The sails fill with a breath of air and tighten.
The boat bends to their bidding.

We cut the motor. A moment of silence, broken
only by the lapping of waves against the hull

and in this moment, silence rearranges priorities.
This exquisite moment becomes our compass rose.

Full sail, in motion, moving ahead.

Below the Surface

Saratoga Passage is calm in the ebbing light
of a winter evening.

The gray whales have returned to Baja
to birth their young.

A duck dips down into the water,
disappears.

I hold my breath waiting for it to reappear
and it does, only to disappear again,

like thoughts that surface and then are gone.
Our lives winnowed down to these moments

of attention, draw us to something beyond
our knowing, something generous, boundless–

the sudden flash of silver minnows,
the half-moon breach of an orca.

Now the water smooths out. A quiet
calmness drifts over the inlet,

yet below the surface an unseen realm
that swims and flaps and splashes.

Voices

The wind does not speak in platitudes.
It always has something fresh to say.

It moves with a whisper that caresses
your cheek and eases a lock of hair,

or a tempestuous shriek as it rounds
the corner of the house, continues on.

Its clear message delivers energy to sailing
vessels, autumn leaves, fragile flakes of snow,

unlike the breath of our words that may circle
the truth, stippled with ignorance or intention.

Timid silences, long-held secrets.
How to honor an authentic voice,

articulate what needs to be said, claim
the power of words like a melody

that finds resolution.

Of Sea and Sky

*In memory of Roger Purdue,
Northwest Coast Artist*

Perhaps his Tsimshian heritage guided
his brush as he gathered sacred images
from the stories of Native people into his art.

His serigraph of an eagle in flight, a salmon
gripped in its talons, hangs in the staircase
of my loft.

The sun rises, a soft peach glow; in the distance
an island shadowed in blue. Elegant wings dip
to the past, rise to the future above a silver sea.

He didn't know, nor did I, when he gave
me the framed print, that soon I would
experience this story of eagle and salmon.

The following week, as I walked along
the shore of Admiralty Inlet, an eagle flew
over my head, dropped to the water and rose,

a large salmon clasped in its talons.
The eagle flew to the bluff and I watched
as the salmon became sustenance for the eagle.

Now echoes bounce from high mountain canyons,
memories of tumbling streams, quiet pools;
ancient voices chanting to a drumbeat–

feel how sky enters the sea,
how the sea mingles with river,
how salmon nourish with sacrifice of body.

Viewpoint

It is snowing, a rarity on the island
and a great blue heron has moved
from the lake into our field to hunt.

A study in patience, it is hunched down
enduring the cold. Perhaps even the mice
and voles are hunkered down in burrows

and here am I, snugged into flannels,
cup of hot chocolate in hand, the twirling
flakes bidding rest.

Plans for outside work abandoned,
I cozy up in my writing room
to consider the lacy flakes

that seem like a gift, as they come
and go, leaving a dainty skim
of white on the landscape.

As I look beyond to the snowcapped
peaks of the Cascades, a sudden coldness
descends as I recall the avalanche

that blasted down the slopes,
took the lives of three hikers
just five days ago.

The Wind's Moods

Living on an island is learning to live
with the wind's moods and occasional
tantrums.

It begins as a hum and you can't tell
if the wind is rousing the evergreens
along the bluff, or provoking waves

that roll in from the Strait of Juan de Fuca.
The hum becomes a thundering voice
of forest and sea, a persistent blow

that increases in intensity. It triggers
an alertness to uncertainty. The landscape
you know can change without notice—

darkness prevails as it confiscates
our power. We realize the turbulent mood
will pass. We will make what we can

of the adventure, illuminate it
with candles and thoughts
of refreshing summer breezes.

Winter Sailing

It was not stormy, but cold and snowing
that day in March. We were bundled
in foul-weather gear.

We glided into our slip without incident.
My husband stepped onto the dock,
line in hand to secure the stern.

I watched him pirouette, reach for a post,
miss, and tumble into the water.
He disappeared.

Seconds mocked me, spinning toward panic
when, at last, he surfaced, stocking cap still
in place, salt water sluicing down his face.

He had hung onto the line, followed it
to its end, realized he was upside down.
Boots filled with air had capsized him.

It's a curious thing, how fear can generate
wild, unquenchable laughter and I laughed
throughout the night.

Spring Storm

Winter storms have settled
their disputes and moved on.
Here on my knees pulling weeds
in the flower garden, floating
on a cloud of spring bliss–
the fragrance of lilac and lavender,
the outrageous throbbing
of crimson peony and purple iris,
a robin startles me as it flies close
by my head. I stand up, wave my trowel.
The bird returns, lands on the fence
by the apple tree and makes eye
contact. It is not a friendly connection,
rather a standoff stare that says,
I'm in charge here. Go away.
This bird is definitely cocky,
chest extended, not a feather
out of place. The bird continues
to fly around me squawking
its objections until I gather my tools
and leave. I believe there may
be a nest in the rugosa rose
near where I worked.
This three-ounce avian storm
moved through my garden,
effectively clearing away human
interference, celebrating spring
in its own way.

Whale Song

Gray whales visit our island
on their way north from Baja
where they birthed their calves.

Islanders say they hear them singing
their watery songs as they travel
through Saratoga Passage.

One came into Penn Cove to feed.
Looking down from the bluff
I saw, through calm, clear water,

the massive shape filtering food
from the floor of the cove, so close
my astonishment billowed into wonder–

a connection so far beyond myself
it became a soul-deep knowing.
I watched as the whale moved away.

Further out in the cove, the whale
breached, a heart-shaped plume
flared from its blowholes.

Unbroken Line

My granddaughter and I like to go to the beaches
that surround our island. She crouches over a tidepool,
lifts a rock to observe the scurry of a tiny crab.

She once found a delicate spiral seashell no larger
than a daisy petal, iridescent pinks and blues and greens
sparkling with silver glints. One can't help
but wonder how this fragile jewel remained intact,
jostled by incoming tides, shifting rocks.

On warm days we dance in the sand waving scarves
of seaweed, sunlight glimmering on briny ropes of kelp,
our rhythm prescribed by the swish and sigh of waves.

It is said if you find a wishing rock—those embedded
with white lines, you are lucky and if you throw
the rock back into the sea with a wish,
your wish will come true.

Sometimes we throw them back, but other times we carry
a wishing rock home, place it by our garden gate.
Legend says, to count as a wishing rock,
there must be an encircling unbroken line,
and what is that, if not love?

II

The art of living lies in a fine mingling of letting go and holding on.
—Henry Havelock Ellis

Reverie

The rhythmical click of the train passing
over rails, the subtle sideways motion
of the car lulls me into a dreamy calm.

We pass by regimented rows of orchards,
apples and cherries replaced by a mantle of snow,
climb into the mountains, rivers and streams
splashing bright jewels into the winter air;
a mighty rush of recycle and renewal.

Along the way, the train carries us through
a long tunnel, eight miles of darkness,
then released into light.

Now, back on the island, the curtains
of morning part exposing Mount Rainier,
a drama wrapped in the colors of sunrise.

Something slippery glides into my thoughts.
I can't quite hold onto it.

It feels like a need to be more than witness
to beauty, to become a part of that which
is beyond; a place to shelter when darkness
sings a sad song.

The Grace of Uncertainty

I glance up and see, high on the wall
of our living room, a crescent moon,
crisp and elegant, centered within
the inner circle of the rose window.

Just a glance, a small thing, but I'm struck
by how the moon and rose window, aligned
by time and space, capture a moment
of revelation.

How graceful architecture, like stirring
words and music, can pierce the shell
of inattention, frame and focus our attention
to something greater than ourselves.

So much I don't understand, and that's all right.
Questions charge the connection to creativity.
A vast mystery shines in plain sight.

If love brought the world into being
isn't that all we need to know?

Beyond Silence

It's a strange thing: death.
You know it's coming
but it still takes you
by surprise. Old friends,
together, we talked
about ordinary things.
Sunlight slanting
across the bed
made the day seem
ordinary. His sons
tended to him,
stroking his head,
holding his hand.
It was beautiful,
really, how they
cared for one
another. Then
silence. I closed
his eyes.

Airy Flights of Blue

Along the coast of Oregon, you can't tell
where sea leaves off and sky begins,
such innumerable shades of blue.

Cerulean embossed high in the atmosphere
wings its way into nothingness. Yet fog,
hovering near the shore, is drawn

to its soft intensity and cascading shades
of blue seep through the clouds' gauzy
netting. It's blue that comforts, just this edge

of melancholy. Only sea stacks,
that jut from the sweep of sandy beach,
remind us of the need for something

solid, a bit of permanence in the midst
of such ethereal loveliness.

Moat of Tears

When grief knocks on your door
you must answer, otherwise
it will just keep knocking.

You won't be able to rest,
nor concentrate on what
you once loved.

It wants to come inside where it can
do its work. If you allow entrance
you may be surprised.

Once inside, grief will begin to unwrap
its gifts. Not an arrogant ruler intent
on keeping you locked in a castle

far away from the land you once knew,
but rather a guide that will lead you back
to a strange but new way of being.

Storm

Whips of lightning crack against the night sky
and a cloak of dazzling light unfurls before us.

Safe on our porch we watch the storm move
toward the island from Seattle,

almost continuous flashes of light, yet thunder
remains a distant rumble, the way worries

are set aside when the thrill of the world
takes over.

We could smell the approach of rain,
the earth rising up to meet the cosmic display.

Resting on the chaise longue, bundled
in a down comforter, a subtle moment

of contentment, yet with the heavens raging
such contentment feels strange.

Perhaps it's the notion of light piercing
darkness that engenders hope,

or the silent streaming of closeness
flowing from those nearby.

Now we hear the rain—large syncopated
drops that somehow promise relief

to what we have held inside.

Gift of Work

It can be a gift or a private kind of distress,
depending on if you've found your purpose.
My friend, a physician and farmer, blends
her two passions into a life of caring.

Leaving her surgical gloves in the treatment room,
she dons leather work gloves when she returns
to the farm. This evening the old work gloves
are nestled together on a bench by the back door

as if one couldn't function without the other.
They hold the form of her hands. The gloves
are dirty, the leather wrinkled, a hole worn
through the tip of the index finger, right hand.

Over years of service, gloves have protected
her hands as she treated deep wounds
in the clinic and in the barn. This gift!
Dare I say, her work fits her like a glove?

Prescription

Sadness tugs at the corner of this quiet
morning; thoughts of a friend, a pharmacist,
now sitting in the nurses' station of a care facility
with a tray and spatula, counting M&M's.

He doesn't recognize his wife or daughter,
but has found his purpose once again–
the steady swipe of *pills*, whisked
across the tray, counted into bottles.

Not all of us find work that satisfies
our hungers, but when we do, the gift
is wrapped in dignity. Perhaps work
is the prescription that restores what is lost.

Penn Cove

This quiet Saturday morning, driving
along the cove, rows of mussel floats
dangle underwater chains.

The bearded bivalves attach themselves,
Prussian blue jewels that foodies prize
steamed in white wine, cream, and garlic.

Twenty-eight hundred miles away,
my friend, visiting in New York City,
finds Penn Cove mussels on the menu

of an upscale restaurant. No posh
restaurants here, the mussels served,
without fanfare, at the local tavern.

I pull over above the cove to breathe
in the salty air. Madrones line the shore,
rusty trunks shedding layers of bark.

A breeze moves through the trees,
gives voice to the syllables of leaves.
Across the cove spring alders

leaf out like whispers against
the sky. At times, ordinary moments
seem enough, as if contentment

comes to rest in the lap of the usual,
but perhaps there are no ordinary
moments, each breath pure grace.

Untold Stories

A small table under a window overlooking
Admiralty Inlet is where I reach for words,
those within and those beyond.
The table is old, put together with square
wooden pegs. The oak is coarse-grained,
wears the badges of age: spills from another
writer's inkwell, a burn mark, perhaps
left from the smoldering ashes
of a gentleman's pipe. The tabletop
is separating, creating cracks between
the boards. Scratches and gouges
polished from use and age leave scars,
yet sturdy turned legs have withstood
the use and misuse of the table.
I laud the scars, now worn smooth,
these emblems of resilience.

III

Knowledge is an unending adventure at the edge of uncertainty.
—Jacob Bronowski

White Peony

Teach me about poetry, she said.
I don't understand.

Perhaps there is nothing to teach.
I can only share what comes out of silence,

how a poet tries to make something
from the rags of this world,

how traumas scatter parts once counted on,
sparking questions, creating something

that wasn't there before, or listening
when the sea sighs as if it carries deep grief,

sorrow released upon the shore. How silence
may offer a sheltering place or a memory

that braids itself through the years. In silence
we become buds that unfurl to possibilities,

how the white peony opens like new love,
how it expands full of light.

Pioneer Cemetery

We traveled the back roads into the foothills
of the Cascades to a tiny settlement
on the Stillaguamish River searching
for the grave of my great-grandmother.

The day was dark, snow and ice sputtering
against the windshield as if to contradict
the exuberance of daffodils that claimed
random patches along the soggy roadway.

A treacherous mountain road, dead ends,
and at last, a lane that led past an old house,
a small neglected cemetery nearby. Blackberry
vines hung heavy on the rickety picket fence.

We crawled through a gap in the fence and stood
in the dense silence of a pioneer cemetery,
a few headstones, tall grass, clumps of damp leaves.
My great-grandmother's stone was easily seen,

an obelisk bearing the name: *Addie May Parker.*
Died October 1892, aged 27 years old.
A wife and a mother of three little boys,
she drowned after falling out of a canoe.

She and a neighbor woman were trying to cross
the river. Here the story becomes wrapped in a shroud
of mystery. I was told she was deathly afraid of the river,
would never have voluntarily stepped into a canoe.

Uncle Bud

He grew up in a motherless home, following
tracks left by a father and two brothers.

A burly guy, welder, truck mechanic,
alcoholic, he didn't gain a footing until

he met Glenna, a vivacious nonstop
talker who encircled his quiet ways

with understanding. I loved to see the way
he looked at her, as if she were a luminous

marker of before and after, all forgiven
and changed by a bonfire of attraction.

The years fell gently upon them until
her stroke, speech reduced to two syllables.

He cared for her, tenderness pressing
into his choices: dressing her in smart clothes,

trips to the hairstylist, his scarred fingers
holding hers as he buffed and polished

her nails to a high shine.

Blue Stilly

We sit by the edge of the river, not far
from the secluded spot we drifted to as kids,
scratched our teenage endearments in the sand.

I watch light filter through the branches of alders,
catch the river's current, seeming to move on, yet
the shimmering glint stays true to its setting.

My husband studies the bridge, noting how one end
is anchored, the other floating to accommodate expansion.
Hooked to our natures, we reflect on different things.

It's a workable combination: He builds things that stand
the test of time. What I do is not always visible.
I'm grateful for his strength, he respects my intuition.

Together we figure it out and move along, sometimes
returning to where it all began.

Homesickness

It's a pull to something familiar
yet far-off, the way the moon
tugs at the tides.

It eclipses the new, a shadowy
unease that slips over the surfaces
of now, like a rumble of distant thunder.

It comes from nowhere and everywhere
all at once–longing intensified
by absence.

Perhaps we must learn a new language,
travel an unknown path, follow the flickering
flame of a new beginning, trusting

that the outstretched hand of the future
may offer compensation that offsets
the ache of loneliness.

The Stone House

They didn't see it coming. Pounding
on the door, a neighbor yelled, *Get out now!*

Minutes later seven feet of mud and river
water rushed through the house taking

everything with it. Both in their nineties,
they escaped unharmed.

During their long marriage they had learned
the art of compromise and adaptation,

were familiar with how the years teach lessons
of loss, yet a sadness wound around her heart;

her wedding ring, which she had placed
in a small ceramic bowl for safekeeping

that morning, was gone. How long does one
yearn for the return of that which is lost?

They did not go back to the stone house.
They gifted it to the lifesaving neighbor.

Two years later, raking in the garden near
the house, the neighbor uncovered

a tiny ceramic bowl filled with sludge,
and embedded within was a very dirty ring

which cleaned up nicely and fit, precisely,
the finger of the elated bride.

Breathe

It started as a day of fun on a Hawaiian beach,
a father and his two little girls. The youngest,

a fair-skinned redhead, wanted to shed her tee shirt
was told, *No, leave it on. Protects you from sunburn.*

The girls played in the shallow water obeying
their father's warning not to go beyond their ankles.

As they played, a rogue wave pounced unannounced,
upon the shore, swallowed them into its belly.

Their father sprang toward the girls, grabbed
the older sister, handed her to an onlooker.

The younger sister disappeared into the churning surf.
Estimating her location, her father dove into the heaving

water, felt her tee shirt, pulled her to him. Both battered
by a determined undertow, he forced her aloft,

each time shouting, *breathe!* Grateful for the thin fabric
of life, we clutch what we love and hang on.

Ring of Fire

We know it's there, yet it's always a surprise
when Mount Rainier's massive presence
appears through a mist of clouds.

It has a simmering heart. We remember the day
its southern sister, Mount St. Helens,
released her tensions.

We heard the boom, two hundred miles
to the north—thought farmers were dynamiting
stumps on a nearby farm.

A drifting cloud of ash darkened the sky,
stopped traffic, piled up on the ground,
confused animals.

Across the cove, we witness Mount Baker's
hot breath gusting from its snowcapped cone
a cautionary tale of high-flung beauty.

These mountains embody strength, gems
in a well-placed crown, yet the throne
is shaky.

Tradition

A quiet woman, she fit into his large Italian family
with the grace of the wind when it whispers through
the trees.

A marriage filled with sunlight, yet the years
were not kind; an eruption of illness spilled into
a lake of deep sorrow.

Family, tradition, affection sheltered them
in a circle of harmony. As each new year approached
they bought a box of Italian chocolates,
the pieces wrapped in blue foil.

Beginning on New Year's Eve, every evening,
sitting together with glasses of wine, they unwrapped
two pieces of chocolate, read aloud the love notes
tucked inside.

Some translated notes were difficult to understand,
others trite. They laughed as the spin of years
made a magnifying glass necessary.

This year, as the Christmas holidays drew to a close,
he weakened, was hospitalized. On January 1st,
before going to be with him, she opened the box,
unwrapped a chocolate, read the note.

A day is as a thousand years when you are not with me.

He died early the next morning.

The Blue Hour

Twilight settles around me cloaked in blue,
as if I'm wrapped in an intense sky.

It drapes over the inlet and flows
toward the sea where the sun,

at a defined place below the horizon,
sends red rays on a mission,

but scatters blue. The spilled inkwell
of night spreads like a gentle spirit,

fills me with longing, a curious
wanting—the need to feel the warmth

of fire, hold a loved one's hand, embrace
what is familiar.

Now a moment when all comes to rest
and the rightness is seen as beauty,

yet as darkness fills in the blanks
a tinge of blue lingers.

Madrone

They are so beautiful in their nakedness,
rough bark falling away to reveal
the smooth coppery skin of the trunk.

They drape over the bank of the cove
preferring the salty nearness of the sea,
shiny green leaves complimenting
winter's bright red berries.

A cushion of dried bark and leaves litter
the ground, a mark of madrones' efficiency,
discarding what is no longer needed.

Their rugged beauty taunts the sky, as if they
had endured hardship, a curious trauma,
yet they flower–sprays of creamy blossoms
like messages of hope.

Leaves in a Windstorm

The idea of getting to know someone
altogether is as futile as trying to gather
leaves in a windstorm.

Like the vagaries of weather, like the shifting
possibilities that energize all of us, how
can we hope to find an unabridged edition?

Why would we want to? Even in bonds
that span years, there are private bogs and dells
not to be disturbed, to be respected.

Our need for closeness burns brightly—a flame
that illuminates who we are, a warmth
that assures us we belong.

Years wrap around our loves and friendships,
enough slack to find comfort, yet bound together.
This morning wind and rain predicted,

but my writing room is filled with light.

Last Hours

These last weeks we talk about how much time
we have left, not morbid, just practical.

My dear longtime friend is at the very end
of her journey. Heavily medicated now,

she still calls and I can't tell if she wants
the reassurance of my voice, or if she needs

me to be with her. I will go, should the clouds
of uncertainty part, allowing me to know the way.

We could always find the truth in each other,
yet now I must bridge the river that runs through

this unknown valley carefully, to be respectful
of her time.

This morning the sky is heavy, dark clouds
pressing down.

We have said all that needs to be said. Now
words are like birds that quiet before nightfall.

In this pure space, how does she wish to occupy
her last hours?

Soft Heart

The old cedar stump spills its soft heart,
through an open wound, onto the ground.

Rings of years unlock their perfect circles
donating a history of hidden stories:

storms and drought, seasons of growth,
seasons of stress.

There's something noble about the old stump,
something beautiful, this slump of decay.

It's almost as if you can smell the fragrance
of forest: flat-needled boughs swaying

in a breeze bearing packets of spiky
resinous cones.

The truth of what was spills out, like a long-held
secret that issues from the deepest part:

green memories of a cedar standing tall.

Sunlight and Shadow

We were careless with our youthfulness.
The two of us, marrying in our twenties,
traveled a road cobbled together
with dreams and aspirations.
We thought it would never end.

We were so immersed in living we didn't hear
the years clicking by. We didn't know
the glow of youth made us beautiful.

The years spooled away like ribbon stretched
across an old typewriter, stories imbedded
one on top of another, marks becoming fainter
with each passing year.

Now memories overhang that cobbled road,
patches of sunlight and shadow. He kissed me
and made me feel as if I were his morning light,
rising to something more than I was before.

He said, *I remember everything.*

IV

Musicians paint their pictures on silence.
—Leopold Stokowski

Next Note

If you hit a wrong note, it's the next note that makes it good or bad.
   –Miles Davis

The jazz guys lean so far into improvisation
that chance becomes a part of who they are.

I admire how they go to a wild place,
no safe space, and make something

of what comes along. It doesn't just happen.
They have churned their way through

the history of euphonies until the present
moment is ripe with choice.

How I wish to be so fluent, to fly
in that freedom,

to make something beautiful
with what is at hand,

to make the wrong note better.

Band of Counterparts

In memory of Gayle Craig

A baton, held high, signals a start and notes
line up waiting for direction. The notes float.
They attach one to another, yet remain pure
to themselves.

They yield to the guidance of the baton,
keeping time with each other—a rousing
march, a band of counterparts parading down
a familiar street.

The director is acquainted with leadership:
a husband, a father, a provider, a friend.
His children, each unique and remarkable,
keep time with each other and with him.

There has been a downward stroke
of the baton indicating completion,
yet melodies remain—as a bell
once struck continues to reverberate.

Hollow

When emptiness
settles like fog

obscuring outlines
of the familiar,

think of a flute, hollow
and simply waiting

to be filled
with breath and air,

as silence gives itself
to song.

Melodies of Wood

Wood, so long silent, comes to life
in his hands, voices that sing, rise
from the acoustic hearts of guitars,
dulcimers, mandolins, and a violin
bearing a mother-of-pearl hummingbird,
poised in flight, on the highly polished back.

Now a guitar: A spruce face, back and sides
shaped from black poisonwood, an exotic wood
when freshly cut, oozes a toxic black sap.
A strip of rosewood, precisely inlaid,
graces the mahogany neck.

On the workbench evidence of how it began:
a stippling of sawdust, curls of shavings planed
from ribs and neck, a forest of clamps,
containers of glue. Fifteen coats of lacquer
before buffing begins.

Near the end I say, *it will be exciting to hear
the first notes,* and he reminds me: *an enormous
amount of pressure must be applied to bring notes
into balanced harmony* and, like parts of life,
he hopes *connections will hold, will not
fly off in all directions.*

The Banjolele

It was a curious gift from my son.
I had never aspired to own a banjolele.

Never heard of one. I wondered
what was expected of me.

As a kid, my time with the piano
and clarinet was acceptable,

but uninspired. Was I now expected
to learn to play an unfamiliar instrument

that stretched its strings between Hawaii
and Appalachia?

After a few days of admiring its adorable
face, I nestled the banjolele into my lap.

I think my son may know me better than
I know myself–

from the first strum,
I was in love.

Night Music

This year I'm eager for the emergence
of spring blossoms. It's not that winter
was particularly hard. Perhaps it's a new
enthusiasm, laying aside previous years
of duties and commitments, aware
that impending grace is not static.

This morning a fairy ring has formed
in the yard, a sudden appearance–
a dark green, almost perfect, circle
that I once thought was caused
by decaying bits of leaves or bark
accumulated underground.

Now, in my newfound musings
about the ephemeral habit of grace,
I have the sense that fairies may have
lingered nearby. I recall,
in *A Midsummer Night's Dream*,
how they love music, how they love
to sing, how their songs lulled
Titania to sleep.

Last night, in the dreamy gauze
of slumber, I think I heard a cello,
a soft drumbeat, and the thrumming
of wings fluttering through darkness.

Keeping Us Humble

Birds stir the air with color and song,
feathered fantasies that linger, variations
on the theme of grace.

Yet, this morning, on the window above
my writing table, a disgusting grayish-black
blob smeared across the glass at eye level,
a bird-sent missive, hardly the inspiration
for meditative writing.

Then a call from my son, a professional
jazz pianist, who related what he laughingly
described as a trauma when an avian deposit
dropped from the sky directly onto his hand
while performing at an outdoor gig.

For all their musical talent and as choreographers
of sky, at times, these companions of the arts
seem more like creative obstructionists.

Jazz Trio

They play on a playground of dares,
risky leaps with no safe landing.

The three speak in a coded language, test
boundaries, color outside the lines,

yet they know how to take turns
and when they take a ride,

thriving on a riff, they turn it on,
an unpredictable trip, composing

in real time—notes reaching for each other,
then taking off again.

We follow along, the beat energizing
 our own rhythms, tasty tidbits of speed—

a celebration of images wrapped
in pleasure.

Forsaking words, they dive deep into choice,
blending options—a smooth cocktail of harmony.

Notes from an archive of artistry linger in the air,
a bird-blue haze that grazes the edge of sadness.

Always an intriguing buzz from a hive of creativity,
separate, yet mingling with what we know,

a cameo of recognition, a taste of something sweet.
They emerge smeared with color and light.

Island Spring

The island is frothed with wildflowers.
Ocean spray, beach peas, daisies, wild mustard,
blue and violet lupine commune along the roadsides.

In the flower garden, fragrances hang in the air
like recovered memories: honeysuckle,
daphne, azalea, peonies, carnations.

New leaves shine with borrowed light
and sunlight animates the bay, a blue bowl
of twinkling charms.

Near the shore, scents from gnarled evergreens
and wild roses waft in the briny sea air,
an opus of freshness.

How to bear such boundless abundance?
I hear a single note from the throat of a bird.
Not *tweet*, but *sweet*.

V

You will do foolish things, but do them with enthusiasm.
—Colette

Original Recyclers

Poets use everything.
We are the original recyclers.

We will find a use for a tin can,
a wilted carrot, a wad of tissue.

Can you hear the music? It seeps
from the trash, the ooze of mud, a crack

in the sidewalk. We marvel at how
a blade of grass curves back toward

where it began and ask why, after it is cut,
it takes on its original shape.

We wade into the mire of sadness, even grief,
and oh, how we love a drop of dew—

its boundless constellations. We hear
ancient wisdom in the *moo* of a cow,

the raucous voice of a crow. We make legendary
soup from the fragrance of rosemary and dill,

paint landscapes from dried-up oils. We overhear
conversations and grab the gab.

If you sneeze around us, we will find a way
to make your outburst blossom into an orchid.

Camano Island Art Tour

John Ringen, Northwest Watercolor Artist

You never know if he's being serious,
his shy sideward glance as he tweaks
words, quietly ordering them to sneak
up behind you and say, *boo!*

His self-deprecating patter bounces
around the walls of his studio, but can't
find a target, overtaken by the sophistication
of his art.

Color invites you in, brushstrokes applied
by a confident hand. The source of this artistry
unmistakable: the artist who rises
each morning, eager to mix paint

with water and passion. Ninety-seven,
eyesight diminished, yet vibrant images
emerge: rushing rivers, stone cliffs, gardens,
mountains, seas, and skies—oh, the endless skies

and you rise into an ethereal realm
where art is a kaleidoscope of captured light,
shimmering color, extraordinary surprise.
Here, among the awards, the adulation

of his students he says, *The greatest gift of all
is to not be able to do anything else well.*

Friendship

The best kind of friend is one who
makes you laugh. The two of us
are not in short supply of endorphins.

She says, *If it's not fun, don't do it.*
I don't know if this is sage advice,
but it works for us.

We turned the hard work of shingling
the house into a metaphorical symposium
on how to fit diverse parts together

in the most appealing way. We organized
a Christmas pageant for seventy kids
into a rollicking adventure that amused us

until Easter. We don't shop in shopping malls
because it's not fun, nor waste our time
trying to make anything perfect.

We travel country roads hoping to find
a treasure tucked away in a secluded
antique shop. We like how simple

country life is compressed into Early
American Pressed Glass. We can set
a sparkling table. Goblets, fruit bowls,

vinegar cruets in flourishing patterns:
Roses in Snow, Kings Crown, Dewdrop,
Windsor Diamond, Heart Plume.

We are especially attracted to antique
punch cups because we know,
Punch cups have been to a party.

Big Bee

Nootka roses tumble along the fences
that line the rural roads of our island,
heavy with the blush and rush
of tender pink blossoms.

They congregate like a church crowd
at the corner of our property,
their fragrance a hymn to the salty
island air.

When our sons were young we frequently
bicycled about the island. I couldn't resist
stopping to push my nose into the center
of the roses, inhaling their heady scent.

Trying to set a pollination record?
my husband asked. The boys joined
in: *Your nose is all yellow. You look
like a big bee.*

The Host

The child laughs, an unbridled,
unrestrained moment of glee
that transfers to me, this pure joy.

I watch him skip across the road
after the last school bell, hopping
and jumping, no plans except to
chase the next bubble of happiness.

This is a kid who has someone
he can depend on, a number-one
person who cheers him on. He breathes
the fresh air of freedom unburdened
by adult concerns.

Be forewarned: Joy is highly contagious—
it finds a host and latches on.

Through Barn Doors

Sunshine through barn doors,
gathering spring trilliums, picking
plump blackberries that seem
about to burst, awakening
to a rooster's tribute to morning,
wading in the creek, polliwogs
in stages of becoming–
a transformation that completes itself
while I feel unfinished, wrapped
in questions from which I've never
emerged. Yet that may be the proper
sequence. Some say the quality
of answers you get depends
on the questions you ask.

Perhaps we are all trying to recreate
the good parts of our childhoods.
After a week filled with heavy
obligations, I found myself
at my father's grave
and it was as if I could lay down
my questions, just be a child again.

Illusions

According to the Washington Department
of Fish and Wildlife, *there are 50,000 coyotes
in our state, occupying almost every type of
habitat, with the exception of islands in the state.*

I look out and see a coyote traveling through
our field here on Whidbey Island.
It lopes along seeming so comfortable and benign
it could be a house pet. Even its pounce, as it
locates a vole, looks playful,

yet I have listened to the mournful
howls and yips of the pack
during the night hours
and recognize the bone-crushing
truth of their frenzy.

I once, on an evening walk, came closer
to a coyote than I wanted to be.
It stared at me from the brambles
that border the road,
eyes of the handsome creature
deceitful and mesmerizing.

Autumn Crocuses

They pop up unexpectedly and lovely,
a pale purple plume of fragile beauty,
yet they seem out of place, celebrating
the exuberance of spring among
the fallen leaves of autumn.

It's like an aged woman who wears
a red smear of too-bright lipstick,
or an acquaintance who feels the need
to sell her home, move from her pleasant
neighborhood because the people across
the street painted their house purple.

Living in the Country

Mr. McGregor got a bad rap.
I am immensely sympathetic.

Weeding in my garden, I find rabbits
have eaten the peas, four types of beans,

and two rows of zinnias. Our home and gardens
are surrounded by verdant fields of grass.

There are even patches of clover. Aren't rabbits
devoted to clover?

They have jumped through an opening
in the fence two feet high

and when that was covered with chicken wire,
they burrowed under.

I'm not easily discouraged, but this setback
has settled on me like an unseasonable frost.

Today, however, the temperature is in the 80s
and the island is shining.

I will continue to pull weeds, concentrate
on how much I've accomplished,

not how much is left to do, and I'll
rejoice—enjoy the beets, Swiss chard,

and leeks that, apparently, are not
the rabbits' idea of gourmet.

Tales from an Apple Orchard

Every Saturday she loaded her three little girls
into the backseat of the car and drove from their farm,
several miles down a gravel road, into Yakima to shop.

On this Saturday the car wouldn't start. Her husband
hooked a rope from his Jeep to her car and pulled
her down the gradual sloping driveway until

the engine turned over. Encouraged, she speeded up,
passed him, the little girls waving from the backseat.
All would have been well except the rope,

still attached, whipped his Jeep around with accelerated
speed and they saw him clutch the steering wheel,
bump over the ditch and sail into the orchard.

Imaginary Friends

They are always available, a bit mischievous,
and eager to join adventures.

As a child, I don't remember having
such companions, but when my sons were young,

they had friends who magically
appeared when called upon to do so.

One son had two companions: Chief
and Peter Anderson. They lived under

the large fir tree in our backyard. Each night
the three had private conversations before bedtime.

The other son also had two companions: Lippy
and Ringer. These friends were married and had ten kids.

They all came to visit one evening while we were
having dinner. Young son let them in

and asked if they would wait in the living room
until we finished dinner. They were quiet guests.

My granddaughter liked naming imaginary creatures:
Shambomb, Drangula, Jocobee, and many other

original, exotic names that were not necessarily
attached to make-believe playmates.

All three, the sons and granddaughter, now adults,
have immersed themselves in creative pursuits.

I wonder if their childhood companions still visit,
whispering encouragements, urging them on.

Desperate Measures

My Swedish husband eats *lutefisk*, yes, he does,
and enjoys it. As a boy, it was served on a platter
of high regard for the Christmas Eve meal.

I once cooked it for him, this pale, gelatinous
fish that disappears if you simmer it a minute too long.
The house smelled like a fish market for weeks.

I admire the Scandinavians who endured cold winter
nights, found a way to preserve their fish by drying,
then soaking it in lye to rehydrate it,

but today, St. Patrick's Day, as I cook a hearty pot
of corned beef and cabbage, I think there must
have been a better way.

Now, each year, we mark our calendars for the first
Sunday in December and attend a lovely *smorgasbord*
at a restaurant near Seattle where the Swedes

and Norwegians fill their plates with *lutefisk*,
boiled potatoes, and *lefse*, all blessed
with the liberal flow of butter.

I dine on Swedish meatballs.

The Sick Tray

Before vaccines galloped in to rescue children,
we took turns itching and coughing our way
through childhood diseases—measles, mumps,
and chickenpox came a-calling for most of us kids.

My siblings and I were no exceptions. We were sent
to bed with stacks of books and a radio to pass the time
while we endured ten days to two weeks of quiet rest.

We called it the sick tray, a small lacquered tray
with brass handles at each end that was used
to carry water, 7 Up, eggnog, and milk toast
as nourishment for our juvenile, bedridden bodies.

All these years later, I am the keeper
of the sick tray. I think about the pathogens
that settled on that tray. It also stirs memories
of warm flannel sheets and my mother
sitting by the side of my bed reading *Heidi*.

We were far removed from that orphan girl
who lived with her grandfather in the Swiss Alps,
but we knew the tender feeling of care.

A Numbers Game

Time swallows the years,
an insatiable appetite,
a carnival of events
with the sweetness
of spun candy,
death-defying rides.
Such whirling, twirling,
a cacophony of barkers
selling claims to happiness.

When the tent flap
is pulled aside,
a wall of mirrors
distorted images
tilted memories.
What happened?
All may not be
as it seems,
yet gliding over
the crest of the wheel
the view expands,
an unrestricted
landscape where more
seems possible.
We stagger under
the weight of decisions,
the airy lightness of choice,
as time makes a perfect circle
of itself.

What We Leave Behind

Some say we have within us,
from the beginning,
a gift of purpose.

As a child I found words planted
alongside flowers. Nasturtiums and lily
of the valley flourished side by side with verse.

Somehow, I wandered into science, tramped
through fields cluttered with equations, chemical
reactions, the mysteries of human bodies.

Are the balloons of joy we held onto as children
still floating? The limitless sky, shifting clouds
couldn't contain our imaginations.

Did the expectations of others cause us
to forget who we were, or were we too young
to hold onto the strings of our passion?

From Woods and Field

That little girl, wavy auburn hair, freckles.
A quiet girl who climbed into the moss-covered
fork of the old maple tree to read,

sought the solitude of the woods: damp
carpet of leaves, the tender shoots
of trillium and bleeding hearts,

the shadowy pockets of secret hideaways,
sunlight blinking through the branches
of evergreens.

She lingered over buttercups that spangled
the fields, logged the magic incompleteness
of tadpoles swirling in the water trough.

She fingered the milk cow's silky ear,
burrowed through dusty hay that filled the loft,
stretched to the rooster's early morning joke.

Her hands packed soil around crocus bulbs,
stroked the first pussy willows of spring, gathered
tufts of baby's breath, adding frill to bouquets.

How long she has traveled, how far she has
reached. How much of what was then,
is in the now?

I hear the little girl calling, a voice
so vulnerable, full of wonder,
bright with promise.

As the years turn, it seems the bud,
once so tightly packed with possibilities,
still unfolds.

Coda

A Fragile Light

Light comes softly through the morning mist,
splinters as it settles on dewdrops that dangle

from the web. Pulled taut and lovely, the web
stretches above a mass of leaves—

green, amethyst, and pale rose.
Silken lines hold fast to spindly branches,

all anchored to the center, geometric
rings of connection, so delicate, so strong

like this catch-all we call life,
how we gather what we think we need

for sustenance, how prisms of light flash
and fade on the fragile structures we create,

how we tremble through storms
holding on, stronger than seems possible.

Gratitude

My thanks to Lana Hechtman Ayers for her insightful editorial direction conveyed with generosity and kindness.

Thanks also to Tonya Namura for her innovative and artistic work to blend the design of *A Fragile Light* with themes that run through the book.

I am grateful to Emily Gibson, friend and photographer extraordinaire, for providing photography to grace the cover of this book.

As always, thanks and appreciation to my family for ongoing creative inspiration and unwavering love.

About the Author

Lois Parker Edstrom, a retired nurse, is the author of two chapbooks and seven full-length collections of poetry, including *Night Beyond Black, Glint, The Lesson of Plums,* and *The Language of Tides,* published by MoonPath Press.

She has received two Hackney Literary Awards, the Outrider Press Grand Prize, the Westmoreland Award, and the Benefactor's Award from Whidbey Island Writers Association. Her poems have appeared in numerous literary journals and anthologies, been read by Garrison Keillor on *The Writer's Almanac,* and featured in Ted Kooser's "American Life in Poetry."

Edstrom's career in nursing and her poetic passion coalesced when her poetry appeared in *Poems in the Waiting Room,* a publication furnished to hospitals and doctors' offices in New Zealand. Her poetry has been translated into Braille and adapted to dance by the Bellingham Repertory Dance Company.

The natural beauty of Whidbey Island, where she lives with her husband, inspires much of her work.

**Other MoonPath Press Collections
by Lois Parker Edstrom**

The Language of Tides (2022)

The Lesson of Plums (2020)

Glint (2019)

Night Beyond Black (2016)

www.ingramcontent.com/pod-product-compliance
Lightning Source LLC
LaVergne TN
LVHW041622070526
838199LV00052B/3212